Because of Poetry...

Also from Shearsman by Kent Johnson

Homage to the Last Avant-Garde

As editor, with Roberto Echavarren

Hotel Lautréamont: Contemporary Poetry from Uruguay

Kent Johnson

Because of Poetry, I Have a Really Big House

Shearsman Books

First published in the United Kingdom in 2020 by
Shearsman Books Ltd
PO Box 4239
Swindon
SN3 9FN

Shearsman Books Ltd Registered Office
30–31 St. James Place, Mangotsfield, Bristol BS16 9JB
(this address not for correspondence)

www.shearsman.com

ISBN 978-1-84861-699-8

ACKNOWLEDGMENTS
Most of these poems have appeared, in varying degrees of semblance,
in *Dispatches from the Poetry Wars*.

'Let Us Now Praise the New American Poetry' was published in the book
Homage to the Pseudo Avant-Garde (Dispatches Editions, 2017). An earlier
version of the late Hiram Addison Jackson's 'To Make an Omelet of Poetry,
You Have to Break Some Eggs,' appeared in *Journal of Poetic Research*.
'Could Someone Tell Me Why' first appeared online at *Dispatches* and at
Best American Poetry blog,

The cover of this book is a work by Michael Basinski, former Director of
the Poetry Collection of the State University of New York at Buffalo.
The piece is titled 'All Because of Poetry, I Have a Big House.'
The art work is owned by Kent Johnson.

Contents

Because of Poetry

Because of Poetry, I Have a Really Big House   11
Poetry Will Save Your Life   12
It's Hard Being a Famous Poet
     1. [THE POTLATCH GIFT]   15
     2. [THE SHOWER]   16
     3. [THE "EVERYTHING IS SO BEAUTIFUL"]   17
     4. [THE GYRE]   19
The Discs of Snow   21
With Fred Seidel, near the Matterhorn, in 2020   23
Dumb Subcultural Rhymes   25
A Review of James Tate   27
The Gunpowder Plot   30
To Those Who May Come After   33

From One Hundred Poems from the Chinese

Overlooking the Great Tidal Bore at Zhang Ridge with Zhang Qiang   39
Near Black Mountain, I Remember Yin Yao   40
On Deer Park Slope, I Recall My Old Friend, Wang Chen…   41
Departing Qinzhou in a Red Army Cart Full of Spring Melons   43
At Five-Forked River, with Mei Yao Ch'en   45
Half Lost in the Southern Mountains, I Finally Arrive…   47
Outside a Dusty Southern Town, I Pause and Write a Poem…   49
At Tan Yuan Ming's Mountain Hut, near Frontier with DPRK…   51
With the Poet Chen Li, at the Sky-View Bar…   54
Three Days after Chen Li Departs…   55

From the Found Journal of Hiram Addison Jackson

To Make an Omelet of Poetry, You Have to Break Some Eggs   59

Let Us Now Give Thanks to the New American Poetry

Let Us Now Give Thanks to the New American Poetry   67

Could Someone Tell Me Why

Could Someone Tell Me Why   81

This book is dedicated to Michael Boughn

—patet luscus, et fortes

Because of Poetry

Because of Poetry, I Have a Really Big House

—to Michael Basinski

Because of poetry, I have a really big house.
Behind the house lives a kindly family of grouse.
They play all around and run, and they flame
All strange, in the specious sun. They are mild and tame,
Of a species where the boy birds sport a mane
Of golden fire and foil. Yes, I enjoy to go for a walk.
I do this much, and as I walk I snort and talk
To myself and sing, like Christopher Smart,
On his knees, O. Hummingbirds and shrike dart
About my head, from which sprouts a forest,
With bats. So, I visit my friend, Ted, the arborist.
He asks me if I want to go to the White Temple
For a while, where they put gauze on each temple
And bring a bluish spoon to take between the teeth.
When I wake, after a dream, I notice that beneath
Me the sheet is brown and wet. Yet Ted smiles
And says, "You did good, Mr. Poet!" And then he dials
His phone to God, and everything again goes black.
That must be when the Giantess takes me in a pod, back
To my house, which is filled with books of fine poetry.
It's funny, says me, that there is no word to rhyme with Poetry,
Except for mongrel slants, like Popery, Coterie, and Ashbery…
Toiletry, says the Giantess, the bully. Her face is umbral Mystery.
Now, on my bed, there's a seven-foot Neruda-faced mouse.
But that's alright: Because of poetry, I have a really big house.

Poetry Will Save Your Life

is a motto I lived with for many years, well, OK,
maybe around six or seven years, from nineteen
to twenty-five or twenty-six. But around that time,
in my mid-twenties, that is, I realized that no, Poetry
will most assuredly *not* save your life. In fact, I said
to myself, it is only making it much worse! I realized
this by looking at my collapsing fortunes and at my
various addictions, accidents, and incarcerations,
not to mention the incident when I shouted a few
lines from Baudelaire and drank, rapidly, a glass of
Drano, which more or less dissolved my esophagus,
so that I have a permanent hole cut into my throat,
through which I must be fed and watered, and
which makes my voice sound like an evil robot's
when I perform readings, which I am invited to give
no doubt much because of my unusual condition,
which makes people feel obligated, as a poet "friend"
once suggested, with a wink, it being well known,
he smiled, that I highlighted my plight in query letters,
accompanied by assurances that I knew their institution
would never discriminate against people with feeding
tubes. Like most poets, that guy turned out to be not so
nice, and this is the other reason I know that Poetry won't
save your life: All you have to do is look around you
at other poets, be it in New York City or some quaint
Midwestern college town and see what unkind, impolite,
and self-involved people they are, the poets, mainly out
for themselves and their "poetry careers," and the bigger
their vitas become, the more unpleasant they get. My third

ex-wife once asked me, and with all her faults, she
could narrow in on a topic and pluck out its essence,
she asked me, "Has any poet even *once* done something
nice for you *twice*, without the good old quid pro quo?"
I wracked my brains on that for a while, and it dawned
on me that no, despite my having done many selfless
things for other poets, mostly younger ones, that none of
them had ever done anything for me more than once unless
I had returned the favor by doing something for them, you
know, the usual things poets do, writing a review or blurb,
putting in a word with an editor, inviting Joseph or Mary
for a reading, stuff like that. And then, when I thought
about it, and with horror, I realized I couldn't recall having
done anything for another poet twice sans payback, either.
This was right before I drank the Drano, which would have
been when I was thirty-six, I think, having realized a decade
previously, as I said, that Poetry would never save your or
my life, so just to clear up the sequence there, as I think I
earlier gave the impression that I drank it in my twenties.
Anyway, it was in my early thirties when I started copying
stuff from Wikipedia and pasting it together and passing
the stuff off as my own work, until I got caught by a mean,
vicious critic, whose article got picked up by a number of
major newspapers and web sites, after which the reading
invitations ended, and so here I am, with my mechanical
voice, writing this poem. Well, the thing to do is to just
soldier on, I say, because at this point, now that I am sixty-six,
what am I going to do, be a gigolo? Maybe I will write a book
and title it *Poetry Will Save Your Life*, a kind of anthology
wrapped inside a memoir, a phrase I saw somewhere,
and which could be marketed by a major publisher as a
kind of self-help manual. On the back cover will be a
picture of me, with the patch over my left eye, a half-

severed ear, and a tube coiling like a vacuum cleaner chord out of my throat. Or maybe no chord. Maybe just the hole. I don't think there's ever been an Author photo with a gaping neck hole, and it would surely go nicely with the title.

It's Hard Being a Famous Poet

1.

[THE POTLATCH GIFT]

It's tough being a famous poet.
All your privacy is gone. It's
enough to drive a person crazy!
Even when people are not coming
up to you at pharmacies or liquor
stores and asking for an autograph,
they are giving you sidelong,
foxy glances, or purposely stepping
into your line of sight and pressing,
quickly, a dark and gristly substance
into their pouty mouths, then
(after counting to three) gagging it
back out, into blue, condom-like
objects, just to get a piece of your
chock-full time and attention.
Granted, those who do the gagging
trick are not normal, common people;
they are other poets. But this does not
make the distraction any less annoying,
not least when they approach you,
smiling, all nonchalant, holding the
squid-thing out to you, as a species
of potlatch gift.

2.

[THE SHOWER]

It sucks being a famous poet.
All your time gets taken up on
the phone or in answering emails
from people asking for a blurb,
and stuff. It's totally tiresome! Even
when young, sexy people aren't
pounding at your door in Paris,
where you're on a grant, you'll be at
the Tuileries, let's say, just walking
around, and someone dressed in a kind
of gold-leaf foil will invariably rush up,
yank your head back by the hair, and
snap a selfie with you. It's sort of like
when the skies over the medieval
college town, where you've been invited
to read, in a vast dining hall, open up and
soak you in this stuff that is like sooty
sweat from the Great War, though when
you look at your hands and feet, they are
a viscous condom-blue, so that you have
to go back to the dorm and take a shower,
in a common shower room, with a bunch
of students and profs with brass chorus
masks who have followed you there, and
you take a shower with all these naked
people in masks who are looking at you
and chanting something you can't even
understand, you know what I mean?

3.

[THE "EVERYTHING IS SO BEAUTIFUL"]

It's taxing being a famous poet.
All your energy gets completely
sucked up. It's so frustrating! People
are always asking you for letters of
recommendation, or inviting you to
do readings, or to teach in Summer
Retreats at Napa, or Naropa, or Naples,
Florida. It's exhausting! Not to mention
the ceaseless invitations abroad, where
you have to give even more readings
than you do in your own country, and
then do long interviews with the press,
which is censored in some of the places
where you get invited, by people wearing
small blue condoms on their fingers, and
where many poets are in jail, and their
books are banned, and even more people
get thrown in the slammer for reading
them, though that doesn't stop you,
for you are a famous poet and must
strive to stay that way, countless folks
are counting on you, and plus, the
honorarium is just too good, it's more
than even the Poetry Foundation pays,
so you go and you say, in this interview,
published in a sanctioned magazine of
one of these countries, where dozens of
poets and artists are locked up, that
"Everything is so beautiful." Though
after a while the pressure just keeps piling

up in your head and soul, so you try to
find ways to get around the ridiculous
demands on your time and space, the way
it all drains the spirit, and so you go to this
reading in your honor, and you read this
long poem that you've copied from the
autopsy report of the poet Liu Xiaobo,
the Nobel Peace Prize guy, who has just died
in jail, from liver cancer, except you move,
for effect, a line from the top of the report
to the end, which is a line that says his
genitals are unremarkable, which is
something the censors sort of like, and
they invite you back next year, too,
to tour with some of the still-living legends
of the "Language movement."

4.

[THE GYRE]

It's tough being a famous poet.
All your creative juices get drained
into answering solicitations from
journals and presses and with traveling
to conferences and with judging book
contests and with doing tenure reviews
for other poets who want to be famous
too. It's just so tiresome! Sometimes it
gets to be so much you just want to pull
a huge blue condom over yourself and
roll down a hill and over the edge of
a sheer cliff, or whatever, and vanish,
until all the glaciers melt again, and
some survivor of the Catastrophe who
is wandering there, hunting for giant
sloth, sees a little bit of blue poking
out from under a rock. But you don't
do that, and you keep your mouth shut
about other things that can't be named
in the Poetry Field, because you know
that the Future is counting on you,
the future of Art. It is tough and hard,
but you must persevere beyond the
pressures and all the silly resentments
of the less famous poets, whose lives
and writing will end up mostly, if not
completely, forgotten, like the fate of
the common people, who live in the
bayou, beyond the University District.
The skies open up above you but it's

not for sooty sweat, like in the Great
War. You are covered in a gold-leaf
light, now, as you head out to the stage,
where four-thousand poets are packed
into a huge room at an annual networking
convention, to hear you recite, in the Russian
or the TED style, without benefit of notes or
book. They are all wearing dark bird masks,
with long, curlew-beaks, pecking rapidly
at some dark and gristly substance that is
cupped in their hands, a tell that indicates
excitement and expectation. And so you
spread your arms and begin, as a wire and
harness pull you above the flock of pecking
poets, and you fly, higher and higher, faster
and quicker, in ever widening gyre, while
the G-forces stretch and flatten your reciting
face, like you're in a House of Mirrors, but
you're not, you're just at a Poetry Convention,
it feels like your face is going to tear off.
It's hard being a famous poet.

The Discs of Snow

"I like the way the flowers grow."
(Jack Spicer, *Billy the Kid*)

I like the way the flowers grow,
The way rain falls, the discs of snow.
I like the writers in my class,
The way they kiss each other's ass.
I wish they liked me equally,
Returning, thus, my fealty.
But Satyr's wage is lonesomeness,
Among the solemn Crotalus.
They coil and fang and hiss away,
At panpipe me, who (just as they!)
Do meekly seek an MFA.
It seems so wrong, so damn unfair;
I want to shear and eat my hair!
I also ponder, actually,
About the role astrology
Hath played in my sad banishment.
Is it perhaps a punishment,
which I incurred in former life,
When I did opt for fascist strife
And broadcast slime in Italy?
Must I pull down my vanity,
A centaur in a dragon world,
Where Prizes fly like flags unfurled,
And followers on Twitter feeds
Predominate aesthetic deeds?
In any case, why should I care?
Let Bernstein have the War Crimes Chair.
The Carriage holds but just ourselves,

And five or six avant-garde elves.
I like the way the flowers grow,
The way rain falls, the discs of snow.

With Fred Seidel, near the Matterhorn, in 2020

*"To our Jewish Guests: Please take a shower before you go swimming.
If you break the rules, we are forced to close the swimming pool for you.
Thank you for understanding."*
*[Sign posted by the management of the Paradies Hotel,
in the Swiss Alpine village of Arosa, August, 2017]*

I don't read poetry unless I have to, which
would be when a guard from Penn is pressing
a knife to my throat in a penitentiary, where I
am residing for protesting some Poetry Institution.
He orders me to squeal, again and again, that I, too,
dislike it, that I wish I were a poet, but I am not.
Well, once I was with Fred Seidel, in the Alps,
at a ski resort, our goggles were plastered in dust,
but we didn't care; we knew the sun, presently,
would melt the white, and our vision be 20/20,
like Gertrude Stein's, in her 20s. The waitress
was a giant. She said: Mr. Seidel, would you sign
my book, kindly, a translation of your Triple
Crowner into Deutsch, by the translator, into Polish,
of Paul Celan? My Name is Heidi, and we do ask
the Jews to take a shower at this Herberge, before
entering the pool, if you will mention this to your
sullen companion, who for some reason is writing
this down, what is wrong with him, it is all most
disconcerting! Yet in any case, and if you will pardon
the dissimilar question, we have always wondered why
you never once referenced Vietnam in your misogynist
poetry of that era. Then she clopped away on her clogs.
We drank schnapps. Fred half pointed toward the great
window: Why, say, that looks just like good old Ashbery
in his 20s! Our goggles were now obsidian and

clear, as the sun was setting behind the great peak,
making this Ashbery figure look quite ecliptic,
with a corona seeming to flicker around his
dark edges, as he bent over a moleskin, writing,
in a fury. Behind him, beyond the glass, rose das
Matterhorn, howling in its hooded grief for the
world. Well, what if it *is* John Ashbery, I said. What
if the war hasn't even started yet? Would you do,
in that case, Fred, what you did all over again?
Not on your life, said Fred, as the man who looked
like his great rival, in his 20s, turned our way
shyly, hopeful, perhaps, or lonely, or maybe both.
Poetry makes nothing happen. It is a dead hound's
lice-filled mouth. That will be €20 million, the same
price of a Poetry building that looks like a bank,
winked Heidi. Thank you kindly for your business all
these years, and may god bless everyone!

Dumb Subcultural Rhymes

—for Bill Knott

In Pyongyang, the winner of the Great National Poetry "Pohoeghed"
[i.e., Award] will have her verses laser-etched on a nuclear warhead.
Now *there's* a poem Commune School poetics can't beat. Dear Ted:
The Language writers are descending; we thought they were dead.
But Frank, Amiri, and Lorine have safely bivouacked the craggy passes,
and with death-defying skills have saved the youngster's too-tight asses.
Let's hope we can tidy up the base camp in time, prepare the folks
a toddy and fair bed. Else, life's the same, here, on the ice-picked slopes.
The east face is swaddled in purest snow, and in the valley far below,
it's solid vetch. When Lorine comes in she makes a belch and says hello,
then cracks her frozen neck. There's no answer for B-B-Being, she stutters,
The hard p-problem of Why. Nor is there answer for the P-P-Pulitzer's
list of finalists the past six years, I mean w-whoa, you know? Bill Knotters
comes up the shining path, dragging ropes and carabiners, screaming he
is in the *New Yorker* just because he's dead, and isn't that just the way she
always goes, for me, in fucking Poetry. We invite him to stop and rest
for a while, to chat with our staff, and cross his hands over his chest,
to fly into himself for a spell. But he just keeps going, doesn't even give
us a glance. He is like a Hell-foam appeared from the gloom, a missive
of Warn. Tiny he grows, ascending into the storm, though his words swell
down the canyons, even after the reception drops from his prepaid cell
doohickey. Anyway, thanks for the card with the moose crossing the road.
It is nice to see that Nature still abounds in North Korea, despite the
      payload
of extinction with said poem. When I coded Liz over Moscow Mules
      at Orwell's
that she would be posthumously glam, she almost chucked up the mussels
and crawfish we'd eaten off fifteen-year-old pages of the *New York Times,*

with pics of little persons jumping out of really tall towers and other signs.
Newsprint's the china at the hot bar in Dumbo, named *Dumb*
      Subcultural Rhymes.

A Review of James Tate

—for Dan Chiasson

The other day I started to read James Tate's posthumous *The Governor's Lake*, subtitled *The Lost Poems*. I liked the book very much. The poems are very nice, they are all in prose, and they meander along, like some forgotten, lost footpath in the Berkshires, which makes the subtitle all the more poignant, and good on the editors for choosing it. The poems tend to launch with clarity and purpose, then drift, before coming to in a fog, far from the blazes of conventional logic or narrative satisfaction. Sorry if it seems I'm overly self-conscious of my prose. A madcap style is the vehicle for implying other, graver things. Iridescent, cretaceous, oyster, cerise, chamois, and more, all of these at once—all words used by Dickinson, in her prime. The jewels are all there; but the real treasure isn't any precious stone, far from it, no. Yes, styles are like trade routes; they fall out of favor, eventually vanish into the sands. But he never cared, and why should he? He rode his loping camel with patient grace and had a flowing headdress to taunt and beat all standard drones. I was reminded, while reading (for what could be more natural than to remember such an occasion?), of the time back in the early 90s, when I visited James Tate in the Berkshires, close to Camp Beckett, where I had worked as a teen. It was really great to meet him, as I had always been a fan of *The Lost Pilot*, which I read when I was at Camp Beckett, actually, and which, again, makes the subtitle all the more poignant—good on the editors for choosing it, as I'd said. It was very nice to meet Dara Wier, too. She is a terrific poet who was James's wife, and because she got her grad degree from lowly Bowling Green State, just like I did, though about a decade earlier than me, it made the encounter extra special. She was very nice, very smart and pleasant, and pointed out this or that species of the many-colored bird-burst at the seven or so feeders they had in the vast and shaded yard: orioles, yellow warblers, goldfinches, purple finches, indigo buntings, spotted towhees, black headed grosbeaks, rose breasted grosbeaks, American redstarts, and the first and only scarlet tanager I have ever seen in my life. What kind of bird seed do you use? I said. The kind that was only made in the lost town of Governor, she said. Where's Governor, I said, I've never heard of it. It's over that hill, over there, straight north, said Dara, and it's been sitting on the bottom of a lake, since the spring of 1897. We got the bags of seed from the last resident-survivor of the town, seven years ago, who happened to be the son of the owner of the town's famous bird seed factory, said James. We inherited about seven-hundred sacks of perfectly exquisite bird seed, said Dara, it keeps forever. The town is sitting on the bottom of a lake? I said. Yep, that is correct, said Dara. It's rumored there are unknown daguerreotypes of Dickinson down there, said James, including two of her sitting on the lap of her Master, locked in glass, owned by an early collector, the town mortician. And scuba divers say that most everything is still perfectly intact, all the old-style business signs on Main Street, and the old houses with their fences and Victorian porches, the school house with its steeple and bell, and the statues of Emerson and Fireside poets frowning in the park of swaying grass beds, he said, pausing from toking on his joint. He looked off over the bluish, smoky hills to the west, with his goat-patch beard and roguish mien. Do you want some grass, he said. No thanks, I said, but thank you for asking, it makes me hallucinate, I'm already seeing an impossible number of songbirds from second hand smoke. Ha ha ha ha ha, Dara and he both laughed for what seemed like seven minutes, or so, until the echoes of their guffaws started to come back, resounding in weird concussions, like ghosts from the hills. Hey, said Dara, wiping her eyes, why don't you and Kent take a hike up Governor's Hill so he can see the lake that covers the lost town like a sheet of glass, ha ha? Sure, said James, ha. So we did. James was tired; he couldn't get out of his chair. So I strapped him to my back with some belts, which he didn't seem to mind, his arms were still free, and he somehow managed, even though we were back to back, as it were, to unhinge his arms from his sockets so that he could stroke my hair, backwards, and he did so for the whole duration of the arduous climb up the hill, softly crooning, in a gravelly voice, There, there, my dear boy, there, there... We will soon achieve the top, do not falter... And, no, of course, falter I did not: The dazzling, emerald lake with the lost town hidden beneath its glass top spread out beneath us, perfectly still and silent, though it was not that large, more like a pond, it seemed to me, though maybe my judgment was off. Isn't it totally neat, said James. Yes, it is really some fucking view, I said. There is a lost species of humpbacked trout in that lake, said James. Wow, I said, really? That's amazing. And then, after a while of my laboriously turning this way and that so that James could also appreciate the vista and comment on it, we headed back down the mountain, though this time James made me strap him to my front, which made it very awkward, perilous, even, to go downhill. But because he was now strapped around my groin, he was able to use his long, simian arms like a pair of extra legs, keeping us, at least, from tumbling down the slippery rocks. Good job, poet! he said, when we finally got back to the gingerbread house from whence we'd come, where he and Dara lived on the weekends, or when they were on seven-year sabbaticals every four years from U of Mass/Amherst. Four legs are always better than two in poetry, though we are like two peas in a pod! he said. Dara was up on the grass roof, in a gauze white dress, helping one of the goats to give birth to Siamese goats, and it didn't seem to be going easy. Did you have a good time? she said above the heartbreaking squeals to heaven. There's goat meat and beans on the stove, just help yourselves! Yes, dear, we had a great time, said James, unstrapping himself from my body, then leading me like a boyfriend by the hand into the gingerbread house. And it is only just now, right at the point where I go into the house, when the plot about the lost lake and the lost pilot and the lost book was totally ready for takeoff, that I realize, looking by chance at the cover of the book again, that the subtitle is not LOST Poems. It is LAST Poems. Last Poems! OMG! All that climb up the ancient basalt or maybe granite hill, whatever, just to pretend like we were flying over The Governor Lake like ghosts or birds or drones. And not only that. The title of the goddamn book is *The Government Lake*, not *The Governor's Lake*. So now none of this book review even makes any damn sense, or is too embarrassing to print. Geez and shoot me now with a blunderbuss. Yes, depressing and a wasted trip, you could say. But even so, I do have to share: Those chunks of goat meat and ranch beans still taste in my mouth-thoughts like the sweetest kisses of Esmeralda. I mean, you tell me, poets, truly. What are the chances, eh?

The Gunpowder Plot

It was complicated digging the tunnels under the Poetry Institution.

But we knew why we were doing it, and we did it gladly.

When the tunnels were dugged, we rolled in the barrels of gunpowder.

Thirty-six of them, though some wented damp and badded, so.

That we had to roll in a dozen more, and it was most hard, for.

The tunnels were narrow and the barrels were large.

They did scraped against the walls we'd dugged, and.

The ancient limestone of the undergrounded came offed in chunks.

With our pushing and pullinged, the crumblings did pile in the tunnels.

Knees were scraped bared, knuckles blooded, backs straineded and bruised.

The heat was infernaling, and.

The stench from the sewer lines of the Institution led us to retching.

We were in a darkness lited but by tallow candles on our heads.

Also, forsooth, there was the fuse-wiring.

Which tooketh four days to get righted!

As each of the 36 barrels had to be connected just so, and.

The fuse-wires drugged backed through the tunnels just so, with.

Little bridges of wood and stone being builteth along the way.

Across the multiplying trickles and pools.

For the limestone was porous and the waters considerable!

Eight of us did this working, while four more stood guardeth above, at strategic spots.

In the great city, feigning to be any kind of normaled person or poet with an iPhone.

Comrade Fawkes was put in charge of guarding, for five nights straighted, the barrels.

We'd shored them right beneathed the teak-wood floor of the vast Events Hall.

Where six young, brave poets, eight years back, had runned for their lives.

Because the cops had been called by the Institution's hirelings, although.

The commandos had done nothinged more than raise two protesting banners.

And shared leaflets to a crowd, in clear and passionated polemic.

The protestors said, Why teak floors instead of writing workshops in the inner cities.

That's when the cops were called by the Poetry Institution.

Of course, no one in the poetry world excepteth a few exiles uttered a noising.

Now we had finished our assiduous working, numb and tattered from our toil.

We bidded goodbye to Comrade Fawkes, who raised, serenely, his fist.

To his wax-dripped brow, in the dear salute of the Republic of olden.

Some of us cried and kissed him on the cheek, or on the lips, without shame.

He told us not to be sad and to remember the world to cometh.

It had all been meticulously planned, the fuses to be lited at 3 AM sharp.

When no soul would be in the giant, bank-like edifice above, so.

That no one would perish.

Though Comrade Fawkes would stay with the barrels until the fateful moment.

Blowing himself to the heavens for the saketh of poetry's sovereignty.

From the insidious creeping of Capital, the State, and the general economy of.

The culture industry, which hath come to invade almost fucking everything.

The explosion was tremendous, shaking the whole Field to its cowardly core.

To Those Who May Come After

—a translucination after Bertolt Brecht

I.
Oh, these are bleak and confounding times!
The casual word is heedless. The unfurrowed brow
Denotes callousness. People pun and prank at this or that.
Mammoths and planes appear in alpine slush.

Yes, weird times inside the diorama, these, in which
Bar talk about vacations and trees is a kind of porn.
For talking like that, one is harnessed to so much harm!
Like the ones who, harnessed-up, leave the Poets House,
Laughing and gossiping past the homeless ones.

True enough: I, too, am a literati-stiff.
But, really, that's just by chance, I swear. Nothing
I do, I suppose, gives me OK to eat my fill.
For some reason they've cut me a break.
(If my luck shifts, I'm screwed.)

They say: Eat and drink, poet, be glad you've been
Spared. Enjoy the diorama! But then sometimes
I think, how can I eat and drink when what I eat
Others cannot, and what I drink others cannot?
(Yeah, I know, it's not 1939, so the language is "off.")
But eat and drink I do, and with a bard's pleasure.

I'd really love to be wise.
The old epics teach us about wisdom:
To rise above the discord of the world,
To be present in the days that one's been given,
Free of anxiety or of fear.
To abide in peace, without hassling others,
To pay unyielding evil with acceding mercy--
The wise don't torture their conscience,
They're happy with their lot, small as it may be.

But sometimes I think I just can't be OK with that.
Man, it's confounding and these days are bleak!

II.
I arrived to the vast cities in a time of bedlam,
Of great heat and extinctions and rising seas.
I came upon my people in a time of terror,
And I rose and rebelled alongside them.
And this is how I spent
The days I'd been given.

I ate my meals inside the terrible trials.
I made my bed among the raiders and the outlaws.
I was one of them, as I had to be, to live with myself.
I got in the habit of loving men and women without bounds.
I looked at the suffering of Nature with fury and fear.
And this is how I spent
The days I'd been given.

In my time, all the roads led to a swamp.
My cell phone betrayed me to the butchers.
I couldn't help it. But without me the comrades
Would surely go on, or so--in false courage--I hoped.
And this is how I spent
The days I'd been given.

Our forces were small. Redemption was so far
Away. So far away it hurt deeper than
You can know. Though, still, it was shining
Like a sun, even if I would never reach it, even
If I chased it like a horse, with all of my might.
And this is how I spent
The days I'd been given.

III.
You who may come after the flood, the hunger,
The thirst, the excess in which we have vanished,
Please think really extra hard
When you speak of our faults and failings,

And of the bleak and confounding times
You've been so blessed to be spared.

For we did what we could, switching our homes
More often than our shoes, all through the small
Poetry wars and the great war of the classes, despairing
At the sins in the latter, and no doubt too much
At the ones in the former. We crossed deserts, rivers,
And seas, and still we never arrived, for we were nothing.

And surely we knew in our hearts:
Even the hatred of injustice
Turns the face into a horrid mask.
Even contempt of wickedness
Turns the voice into a growl! We
Who yearned to lay a foundation for tenderness,
Could not ourselves learn to be tender.

But you, where you are, in a time and place we can
Never know, where you may live lightly upon the earth,
We hope, in a greater mystery now, and confusedly
Pleased: Please think of us with a simple measure
Of forbearance and compassion.

From:

One Hundred Poems
from the Chinese

Overlooking the Great Tidal Bore
at Zhang Ridge with Zhang Qiang

Horsemen stream from the 复合gate.
Hazy sun hangs far in smoke-filled air.
High tide roars from the great iron bore.
The new DNC of Poetry rules the roost.
Mainline and Avant covet the power
centers of administrative culture. The
Poetry Foundation is a labyrinth of State
and Corporate passageways; they branch
for hundreds of miles under the ground.
Two years a minor official in Chang'an,
personal secretary to Robert Creeley, I saw
my share of court conspiracy and intrigue.
Now, driven here from the clear-cut peaks
(fetid rags, hair matted), the wild, toxic
greens I've come to crave leave me hungry,
at Literary Buffets of the Imperial Hyatt 帝国.

Near Black Mountain, I Remember Yin Yao

Wind drives, knocks hail around in thick pines.
Currents rush, gold-leafed, through conglomerate
clast. Woodcutters come down from the peaks,
cry-out and laugh, butt-naked, in freezing pools.
While my hair was cut straight across my brow,
you came by on pink polyvinyl chloride stilts,
playing horse. In red evenings, we tied tight
bands around our arms and ate 紫色 plums.
The Frigidaire gave off weird clanks and hums.
Where have you gone? To Chang'an, or Luoyang,
perhaps Spokane? The Field's in an interregnum,
sort of like the 18th Brumaire; it's all happened,
as they say, super-fast and by stealth. What
marks this upstart poetic ruling class as Event
is the Big Tent, Third Way nature of its canny
putsch (crucially aided by Capital gifts), likely
tweaked by intelligence ops, with aim to cloud
the classic, simple power flows of the 清朝,
thus, tying bands of confusion around the arms
of anti-Culture Industry insurrectionists to come.
There's a cozy, biddable Coalition, now, a kind
of neo-PC-Cop mandarin court, and the Game's
the speculative division of insider-traded, low-
risk grants and bonds. I admit I've grown old
and surly. My liver is shot. Almost all the friends
of my youth have abandoned me. If you're coming
down through the narrows of the River Kiang,
give me a ring, my cell is 815-234-8004. I'll
come out to meet you, as far as Cho-fu-sa, by the
mist-shrouded ruins, on deserted Black Mountain.

On Deer Park Slope, I Recall My Old Friend, Wang Chen

Back from the gym, I drink from the well.
Evening clouds are mauve, hackle-wisped.
New moon's a whetted sickle. You angled
an oxidized hammer over it, playfully, for me
to see: Long live Chairman Mao! Then we sat
on the busted porch, opened a growler of baijiu,
from the good-old days, before the Great Leap
Forward. Five-toothed toasts and you're off,
in your wild grad-school style, which hasn't
changed, even as it never failed to get you in
big-time jams with the poetic Red Guard, not
least the welt-webs of scar-skin on your legs.
Essential to the opportunist denouement is the
诗歌基础. The grand Coalition of careerist
cliques was much boosted by the institution's
lawyered birth in wake of the $100+ million
opioid Lilly gift, now worth around $200 million,
or so they say. It sounds paranoid, but I don't
think it's merely accidental: Note that the first
two Presidents of the 诗歌基础 have announced
their past links to the banks, the energy sector,
the State Department, the CIA and NSA—both
of them have been advisors to the security
agencies, it's right there on their public vitas.
(I put my finger on your wet lips, whispered
that my neighbors, Y** and Y****, both
Chancellors of the Academy of Police Poets,
might hear.) Drunk now, you just got louder:

And a bunch of other establishment reps, with
who knows what connections, were brought in
to sit on the Board! $#&*%##!!>~@*=$^+!!
A zest for the fields and moors stirs in us still.
The ambition for robes of office has long since
turned to loathing. Today, I got an email from
an old pal, who told me his students at Brown--
POC and Caucasian both--pretty much want
all white people over forty to beg for mercy
on an Elizabethan rack. How are the anti-
Stalinist communists doing these days in
Yangzhou? Say hi to them for me. Does
Lorine yet live on a spit, in Fort Atkinson, WI?
Is Axel's Bar still there, on Oakland and Locust?

Departing Qinzhou in a Red Army Cart Full of Spring Melons

I've grown plodding in my fading years.
My common tasks become more and
more labored. In toilet care, I strain. In
dressing, I can barely put on socks.
What unforeseen toil the years do
bring! What humiliation!

OK, in this dream I'm departing
Qinzhou in a Red Army cart full of spring
melons, bouncing along, with Liu
Xiaobo's *Za Zuan* on audio. It's a sure
and cruel sendoff for the aged:
A virtual poetry Bank is founded to buy

poets off, to create one Big Tent,
wherein everyone "gets along." The
Paris Review, cloak-and-dagger with
CIA, was vanguard of U.S.-lit soft
power in the 50s and 60s; The Poetry
Foundation, its loaded legatee,

has bosses who blithely brag of expert
ties to Wall Street and the Intel agencies
(not that such much troubles most lib
bards)! Granted, the selloff started with
the general recouping of the Po-left
into Academe, circa

mid-to-late 80s. Later, the Poetry
Foundation swabbed up lumpen Avant
surplus for cheap, on auction block. It's all
pretty much a bought, cheerful Duma now:
The residual Middlebrow Mainstreamers
on the right; the opportunist

Liberal Innovators on the left; the
insurgent POC/PC arrivistes in the
center, tacking to and fro, and with
breathtaking skill, sailing
the Rules of the Game. What's to be done?
Bolinas is condo strata. Nanluoguxiang's

a Po-bourgeois tourist-trap. The whole
Field's been cop-linked by laptop. How
bewildering and deeply disseminated, the
fathomless clouds of 天堂之河... How
bittersweet, these spring melons
in a Red Army cart departing Qinzhou.

At Five-Forked River, with Mei Yao Ch'en

All passions come to dust. Great cities sink
into clay. The streams don't care. The
grasses don't give a hoot, either. At dusk,
when owls call for love, petals are falling
like a girl's robe a thousand years past.
Well, said Mei, taking a long chug, then
handing me the jug, the decided drift
of "experimental" poetry in the U.S. has
been, for the past forty years, or so, towards
the smug, esoteric, quasi-teleological range
of affect, its adepts sporting their crème de
la crème presumptions with an importance
of being earnest little seen since the fin de
siècle. Albeit without a guiding temper of
satire and wit to comparably recommend
it, etc. The tendency at issue is fairly
contrary, safely said, to basic senses of
the vernacular and polemical, which we'd
been discussing. A fair number of these
writers are terrifically gifted, to be sure, but
that's neither here nor there. The moon hangs
in the vacant, wide constellations. Pine cones
drop in the weedy garden. Why are Amiri
Baraka and Ed Dorn both weeping and laughing
at the same time, in the corner over there, by
the cash bar, Suite #1989? Muriel Rukeyser
rushes from the shack and bellows a fit
for the ages when she sees what has happened.
Too late, too late. The 番泻叶 bushes bloom.

The water roars as it has since the very beginning.
The same clear glory extends for ten trillion miles.

Half Lost in the Southern Mountains, I Finally Arrive to My Lodgings, Where I Am Startled by Mei in an Ancient Room

The path up the mountain keeps fizzling
out, in the jumbled rocks and scree. When
I see the monastery, huge bats are already
feeding in frenzy. I go to the guest room
and sit on its gilded veranda. The rain has
stopped. The clouds are torn and red. The
gardenias are aflame. Helen Adam comes
up and says there are ancient paintings on
the walls. She goes and gets a Coleman
flashlight. I see they are incomparably
beautiful, especially the ones of Robert
Duncan and Robin Blaser, as painted by
Jess. Then Mei, whom I'd lost in the mists,
begins to speak, like a ghost, behind me.
"It used to be that heterodox poetry, at least
in the U.S., had some serious interface with
the quotidian, and was more all-embracing
for it. Think of Whitman and Dickinson and
Williams and the Objectivists, for instance.
Or of the NAP era, not so long at all ago--
so informed, across its groups and strains,
by everyday life, demotic language, and a
decidedly non-professionalized sociality.
But that down-to-earth ambience of the
field more or less went poof with the ascent
of Language poetry and its obsessive conflation
of poetic vocation with theory à la mode, much

of the latter of pseudo sort, we now know."
The figures glow from within. Helen Adam
spreads our bed and sweeps the mat. She serves
us kidney pie and 粥. It is simple Scottish
fare but fair and fine. The night goes on as we
lie with our hands clasped behind our heads,
loafing at our ease, listening to the great peace.
Crickets chirp and click in the night. The pure
moon rises over the ridge and shines on the
fresco of Kenneth Rexroth on the wall. He
looks mad, now sad, depending on the fickle
shadows of the trees, swaying in the wind. At
daybreak I get up alone. I saddle my mule and
go my way, down the face, letting Mei sleep
and snore like a hibernating 熊. The trails are
fucked, all washed out. I go up and down, the hail
clanking on the mess kit at the saddle. I pass pines
and oaks ten men could not reach around. Where
have the anti-careerist poets gone? What has
happened to their dreams? Will anything like
the 50s and 60s come again? Mocking macaques
snicker from the trees. If I only had a few friends
who agreed with me, we'd retire to the northern
mountains and vanish, like Lew Welch, for
always, without reason or trace.

Outside a Dusty Southern Town, I Pause and Write a Poem, Thinking of the Great Departed Poet, Ch'iu Chin

Who says the dead don't think of us? Certain
surveillance cameras at cultural conventions
show they stand in line behind us, snorting or
stomping, passes in hand. Sometimes you can feel
a small poke on your butt, when there is no one in
line behind you, at all. The dead whirl round in a
bluish light. In addition, they are crevasses transverse
to flow; steeper slopes cause them to slide faster.
Not that we don't want theory. It's that now, much
due to the overdo, "avant-garde" verse has moved
on to get conflated, rapidly and willingly, with the
Academy and mainstream print venues, to the point
where we haven't had an institutionalized habitus
like it since the New Criticism. Penn is the new
Kenyon, and the prominent Presses, Literary Prizes,
and State or Corporate Fellowships leash the values
of attention. A full moon rises over the *New Yorker*.
Evening sunlight and autumnal colors shine on the
Guggenheim's carapace. Where once *Floating Bear*
and *Fuck You: A Journal of the Arts* got cranked
out by kids who shopped at Catholic Charities, track
lighting comes on in $3 million Soho studios. Now,
most young poets shop at GAP or 相关的写作程序.
Shuttled through shafts and ducts of Yves Klein Blue,
they blithely pursue highbrow and recuperated stations,
in fashionable modes and synthetic dispositions.
Recently, dead-by-its-own-hand Conceptual Poetry

showed us, and with insufferable Warholian hauteur, the clearest, most cynical acquiescence to these ideological conditions, even as the group's hipster practitioners proclaimed their winking devotions to the ordinary and prosaic. The Eastern Cantons are full of grinning cops. A virtual Poetry Bank exists to buy poets off. When I dream, everything is as it used to be: The living are the living. Yet when I wake, I am returned to the land of the stomping dead. Here come two young poets with books from Wave, drawn in a cart by J. Spicer and J. Kyger. The poet-horses have gold bits clenched in their foamy mouths. The cart-poets whip them, again and again. *Why? Why?* Poor horses! I want to throw my arms around their wet necks and sob until I go mad. Major or minor, the dead are together as pure souls.

At Tan Yuan Ming's Mountain Hut, near Frontier with DPRK

1. Snow clouds mass over peaks; blossom-viewing Shi
2. Club's in peril. Tan and I sip snow-water at cliff's
3. edge, reciting Pound trans. of shi from the Tang. Trees
4. burst blossoms like on scrolls. Spring freshets mass on
5. perilous cliffs. Scrolls and blue clubs of Tang stuff
6. are buried in scree of wild hills. But blue glacier's long
7. gone. The Emperor is full of shi*, *stet*. DPRK firestorms
8. mass dark clouds over hills; old growth's burned, pale-dark
9. lit scree [check] blue or black. Red Bards tweet cash bar,
10. Rm. 271 for toast of fresh Anthology of Flarf Club (Edge),
11. Ed. by upstart Chancellors. Will lead-edge kids have new
12. burn among 死山garde? Yan'an Academic Rectification
13. Movement's in full swing; Post Guard's lit up, commands
14. united front with panicked rear-garde of pale Prizes + Lit-
15. Cult ISA stuff. No question rectification long in order. But
16. arrears, now, it's race to panic-line, with Trials and stuff.
17. Some people are toast, as in black ash, like kids in DPRK.
18. Prize-vines of Academy 死山 flower-hang hundred orders
19. long from cages; Chancellors take a drive, eye essays for ISAs
20. on fake "hoaxes," inspect true flowers or birds in Po park.
21. At cash bar (said Tan), they do shots with blossoms & snow-
22. water, also rare birds of 18th century, when panic of hoaxes
23. crashed Augustans, no doubt in partial cult riposte to new
24. versions of English copyright laws, the Ashbery Edict, for
25. one, not to mention German Romanticism, which probably
26. doesn't even happen without MacPherson and Chatterton.
27. Bunk: *Race and the Racist Hoax of El Ingenioso Hidalgo*
28. *Don Quijote de la Mancha*, by Cide Hamete Benengeli,

29. published by Mongrel Co. and Harriet Ed., finalist for
30. NBA, NBCCA, and NKVD awards, argues more or less
31. 70% of novels and published poetry in UK and America
32. over last few colors of 18th cent. were anonymous, pale,
33. or pseudonymous, and in first three colors of 19th a good
34. 50%, like mongrel blue. Also, many Prize-winners after
35. all colors. 50 to 70% of readers were hot; also, Benengeli
36. texts, colors went 60% for this: Pleasures of apocryphal
37. lyricals and fictionals were not just texts, but more or less
38. hot mongrels, aspects of reading cult way more chill spec.
39. on attributional indeterminacies than cult uptight bird dune
40. now. Young peeps were fine and cool specked on who the
41. trans kids be—what trace, or clue to birds might be hard
42. though cool-relaxed. That's really interesting, I said. River
43. flows dark in snowy sun. Also, said Tao, lighting Gauloises,
44. Blue glacier's not actually gone. It's stored in vast basement
45. of Poetry Foundation, tended by upstart Chancellors, where it
46. silently circulates superfluid helium around LHC's accelerator,
47. ring keeping bunk at minus 271 degrees Celsius. Wow, I said.
48. Red and green superfluid birds flash over river, eating blue-
49. winged olives, flash shade-gleam on water. When Pound
50. writes that "He bites through the flower pistil and brings up
51. a fine fountain," what did he accelerator, sort of? It ideology
52. both sexed and sort of creep-LHC, *stet*. UFOs appear, disappear
53. on fighter-jet cams. Kids in Congo wave stump arms, thank
54. you, avant poets. Bridge-head glitters against creep, like, pistil
55. sort of occluded sun-head. Headgear's hung on branches of
56. pine in small wood. Horses neigh, while troops do sun-sex
57. contest on really old laptops, purposely burning own lips
58. and limbs, with white-hot boughs of head-pine. Studies show
59. illegal mimeos of Langpo shi circulating in Chinese were
60. giant impetus for Tiananmen. Affirming it, as ancient sun-

61. sex trumps do it, same old shi*. Paradoxical, everyone
62. both pines for Trials and is really cored to death of Trials.
63. Everyone's cored, I guess, so all's OK. Sorry for clichéd
64. closure, but you know you know in bones U.S. Po's totally
65. trump trans with giant invisible Author at core.

With the Poet Chen Li, at the Sky-View Bar, atop the CCTV Tower

At the very top of the CCTV Tower, I visit with poet Chen Li.
Each table has an arrangement of tortured irises and pebbled
bays. We have a drink from Wisconsin called an Old Fashioned.
The city is drunk. We have four more. I tell him his sexy poetry
sucks. He tells me he doesn't care what I think, that I can go
masturbate in Yellow Jade Quarter, under the six-lane autobahn to
Tongzhou. We go on like this until closing time, making toasts,
exchanging pleasantries, and laughing, two old men who love
one another. The hot courtesans of the night, boys and girls,
pay us no heed. We know that when mountains had wings the
scourge among gods was to amputate them. Then, the conditions
within the subducting slabs as they plunged toward the mantle in
whatever zone of the old quarters also produced strange regional
effects, characterized by paired metamorphic belts, whatever. Like
the two of us, feeling our souls entangled in cross-cut strata of
friendship. Of course, our poetic jealousy and competition know
no bounds. Duo Duo licks boots. Shu Ting covets the game. Hai Zi
is a stale joke. Language poets are agents of the MSS. What has
become of poetry's noble line? Where are Lorine Niedecker and
Li Shang-yin? The Changbai mountains burn from great Korean
fires. The blue-porn strobe, at top of the Tower, makes Chen Li
a spook from the late Tang, or maybe the Sung.

Three Days after Chen Li Departs back to Hong Kong, a Venerable North American Poet Arrives to Meet Me at the Sky View Bar, High above the City, at Top of the CCTV Tower. After Many Years of Email, We Are Delighted to Make This Acquaintance. He Is in His Early 70s, but Looks No More than 60. He Tells Me a Story about His Poetic Youth, and I Write Him the Following Verse on My iPhone 8: 天堂是一个万年前流浪的鬼魂

There was a time when I almost moved to Bolinas, he
said. Jack had introduced me, and Joanne was encouraging
me. I was out of grad school, jobless, footloose, ablaze.
When I went to visit for the first time, this is true, I was greeted
at the edge of town by a young, naked woman on a horse. She
invited me to ride, but I was in my car, a '79 Mustang, in fact.
So, I kept going down the sandy road, like a kind of centaur,
with a bunch of books and manuscripts jammed in my trunk.
What could I do? I bumped along the road towards the sea.
Creeley was adamant that I should not go. Joanne told me a
story of Creeley on his hands and knees in the Bolinas marsh,
puking his guts out. Soon, he would split for Buffalo and
turn on Olson. I don't quite remember what happened after
that. Everything changed at great velocity. But here I am,
in China, with everything paid for, if I wanted, and sometimes
it feels, now, like my whole poetic life has been a dream, one
of those that feel like hours, even years, though when you look
at the clock, you see only a few minutes have gone by, like in
Blade Runner, or something. But if I know one thing in the end,
after all this time, it's this, and go ahead and laugh, if you want,
I know who I am and who I don't want to be: *I'm not letting
anyone buy my goddamn way.*

Thus, the Sky View bar turned slowly in the sky, on its Alibaba wheel. A robot trolley, made by Baidu, arrived with our bluish-green gins. We slid cards into a plasma slit and were thanked, in 3D, by a sexy courtesan of the Ming. I typed a stanza on my iPhone 8, from a poem by dead Liu Xiaobo, set the Voice-Trans app to high, and pressed it to the white ear of my American friend:

My dear poets, here and there,
today and long ago,
Paradise is a wandering ghost,
for ten thousand years,
before it will be born.

From the Found Journal of Hiram Addison Jackson (1983-2015)

[nota bene:
On the cover of the journal (found by the poet's fourteen-year-old daughter, Beulah, in Tupelo, Mississippi, shortly after his passing, and given to me because of my correspondence with Jackson in 2013) is the following sentence, scrawled in red marker, across the cover: "To Make an Omelet of Poetry, You Have to Break Some Eggs." The entries have been selected, partially reordered, and edited for punctuation and spelling.]

To Make an Omelet of Poetry, You Have to Break Some Eggs

1. Did block me on her Twitter.
2. Did Unfriend me on the Facebook.
3. Did kick me off a poetry Listserv.
4. Did humble me badly on the Instagram.
5. Did done blocked my email.
6. Did wrote my boss at Starbucks saying I was a "troublemaker," that I didn't clean my hands after using the commode and that I even did drink from the commode.
7. Did said in a meeting of the *Boston Review* that he "hated" me.
8. Did said she desired to send me some "good anthrax" in the postal.
9. Did done actually called the cops on me for merely standing outside her window, wailing her precious name in my pain.
10. Did done actually called the cops on a bunch of young peacefully protesting poets at the big Poetry building, now what poet could have been so diseased in his or her heart to do that?
11. Did call me a Bespauler and a Babolyne.
12. Did unkindly delete all my comments on his blog.
13. Did threateneth to unseemly sue me.
14. Did actually sue me.
15. Did done blocketh me on Twitter.
16. Did done blacklisted my good name.
17. Did useth the tape of a 1970s debate I was in with a famous poet, yet without my permission in copyright.
18. Did put up flyers about me on the campus, claiming I was a "pedophile goat with crabs."
19. Did blocketh me on Twitter.
20. Did done organized a character assassination campaign against my good name.

21. Did wrote a bad review about my poetry out of purest spite.

22. Did gossip maliciously about my good name.

23. Did done lied about me to the ends of the earth.

24. Did encourage others to never answer my emails nor my postcards.

25. Did done threatened to report me to the Security Services in Tupelo.

26. Did done said I was a Drate-Poke and a Driggle-Draggle.

27. Did kicketh me off a poetry Listserv.

28. Did wrote me a note that sayeth, Don't let the screen door hit you in the ass on the way out.

29. Did wrote an essay saying I was full of "White Male Rage."

30. Did done humiliated me on the Instagram.

31. Did wrote an essay saying my chapbook, all of whose copies were sewn by my sisters, was the "case study of when everything goes bad for mentally ill poets in Mississippi."

32. Did done called my mother anonymously and said she never should have born me, You worthless Yankee slut, she said to my poor mother, who never hurt a flea.

33. Did done threateneth to kill my cat.

34. Did unseemly slept with my former wife, which is why I sought recompense with the derringer, and of this I do not repent.

35. Did said she would tell everyone I voted for Trump, even though she knows I merely abstained because Hillary is in the pockets of the big Yankee banks.

36. Did done Unfriended me from the Facebook.

37. Did slept with my former boyfriend.

38. Did done Unfriended me from the Facebook (this happens commonly, as you can see).

39. Did slept with my former girlfriend.

40. Did slept with my father.

41. Did done blocked me from their Twitter.

42. Did slept with my daughter, Beulah.

43. Did done claimed I was a Gnashgah and a Gobermouch.

44. Did bumped me off the National Book Award long list.
45. Did lobbied against me being on the National Book Critics Circle long list.
46. Did done sprayed bear mace in my drink at a cocktail party for rich Yankee poets.
47. Did blocketh my email.
48. Did done pretended to fall asleep at my reading.
49. Did Unfriend me from the Facebook.
50. Did done actually fell asleep at my reading, in a snoring.
51. Did tied me up and burned my chest with a lit cigar, the snake.
52. Did put me in a coffin box and buried me alive, the scoundrel.
53. Did done stole the idea of my poem and published it as her idea, the wench.
54. Did shot me, thrown me in the trunk of a car, and then cut me up into small pieces, middle of the night, in a foul smelling copse, north of Mobile, the *New Yorker* bounders.
55. Did humble me badly on the Instagram.
56. Did done called me a sexist and a prude, an interesting combine of insults.
57. Did done Unfriended me on the Facebook.
58. Did suggest I was the Jeffrey Dahmer of poetry, even after I promoted his poetry to the skies.
59. Did called me a "feckless bitch."
60. Did put her diseased spit into my drink at Orono.
61. Did done squeezed his acne pimples and saved all the pus, then mixed it into my latte, while I was in the toilet at the Hyatt, between panels, and for no other reason than jealously at my Pushcart nomination.
62. Did done called me a minor poet, what a joke, I don't claim to be James Dickey, but she's one million times more minor than I!
63. Did done said he'd give me an 'A' if I'd pee on him all over.
64. Did said I needed to "get some mental help."

65. Did left pornographic comments on my Facebook in Hungarian, using the translation machine.
66. Did imply I was a Rakefire and a Saddle-Goose.
67. Did tied me to a bed while I slept and then broke my legs with a baseball bat, before bringing a razor blade into the room and sawing off my you know what, while reciting Beowulf.
68. Did spreadeth "not-nice" gossip about me, and all over the county.
69. Did make fun of my "porn" moustache, as they called it.
70. Did done unfriended me from the Facebook.
71. Did wrote my publisher, to say I'd forced myself on her, when it was she who had unseemly bellowed, three days fore, on our anniversary, completely out of nowhere, the two of us just sitting there pleasant (and after I'd given her a set of ear-rings to celebrate her first published poem), that she hoped her secret boyfriend would take me cuffed to a cabin out in the woods, where five meth heads would rape me and then put a rabid mouse up my rectal.
72. Did refuse to acknowledge my Friend request.
73. Did done looketh at my crotch, I think, at a reading.
74. Did shouteth I was a Scobberlotcher and a Snoutband.
75. Did done blocked my email.
76. Did done spread gossip about my penis after she'd accidentally walked in on me in a collective shower room, in China, where we were on avant-garde reading tour, paid for by the generous and kind Chinese government, and the shower room was freezing because it was winter and the heat had gone off, and so my penis was the size of a button mushroom, but she thought this was the normal size of my sex, so she went and told a whole bunch of people at her program about my "button mushroom" penis, over email, and she did this, I'm sure, because I have more publications than she has.
77. Did glance at my breasts, I think, at a cash bar, AWP.
78. Did humble me badly on the Instagram.

79. Did done sayeth she wanted to set fire to my house while my family and I were tied up inside, screaming for God to please save us.

80. Did unkindly make fun of my man boobs and love handles.

81. Did done sayeth I'd never have a career in poetry after I said something critical about Language poetry on a Language poetry Listserv.

82. Did wrote a long review and said something about everyone in the anthology, except for me.

83. Did refuseth to help me get me an interview at the AWP, even though I helped him get maybe three.

84. Did Unfriended me from the Facebook.

85. Did done refuseth to invite me to read at his college, even though I'd invited her twice.

86. Did done say that if he had one wish it would be to burn down the village of my ancestors in late 18th century Maine, after having scalped everyone with the help of Native Americans still loyal to the Crown, so that no one after 1798 in my lineage would be born, least of all me.

87. Did blocketh my email.

88. Did unkindly scream I was a Muck-Spout and a Mumble-crust.

89. Did done said he would like to tie me to a chair and force me to slowly eat the roasted, blistered corpse entire of a certain corpulent American President, lest penalty of the torture-death of all of my children and relatives, immediate and distant.

90. Did wrote a very bad review about me just to soil my good name.

91. Did said mean things about me in workshop, even though I slept with him, doing the most unspeakable acts, just to satisfy his disgusting longings.

92. Did stood me up in Sarajevo, on purpose, even though I'd invited them to go there with me.

93. Did block me from her seven Twitter accounts.

94. Did done plagiarized me in the *Denver Review.*

95. Did done blocked me from his Twitter account.

96. Did sendeth me postcards from springtime Paris, the notes dripping with aggression, asking me, for example, how things were, back at Tupelo State.

97. Did plagiarize me again (a different poet) in the *Denver Review.*

98. Did plagiarize me in his hot book of anti-war poems a few years before he won the National Book Award for a second book of anti-war poems.

99. Did done Unfriended me from the Facebook.

100. Did put a piece of big wood in my pillow, at a poetry conference in England, which nearly broke my head.

101. Did done never even thanked me for the review book copy I sent her after I'd reviewed her book on my Facebook page.

102. Did the water-board on me in the secret basement of the $23 million big Poetry building, and because I never gave them any names they put a plastic bag over my head and asphyxiated me, a horrible death.

103. Did said she'd interview me for an important journal and never did and probably never intended to, I realize, now.

104. Did done put a cherry bomb into my cat's ass and lit it.

105. Did hiss I was a Wandought and a Yaldson.

106. Did done told me they'd never even heard of my poetry before.

Let Us Now Give Thanks
to the New American Poetry

Something happened to me at the waterpark.
—Allen Tate

Prelude

Not that anyone would or should
care for my fickle poetic leanings,
but I've elected now to share, half
naked and pickled as I'm presently
feeling (I'll explain), some thoughts
about some things, that these thoughts
might flutter about, with errant and
rowdy wings, while the mind is juiced.
So to begin and without further fanfáre,
I'll just say so: that Mayakovsky and
Vallejo, fair poets of the hammer and
the sickle, are pillars in my heart,
without compare. And yet on other days,
alas, and at prevalent spells for near a
week, or two, I will seek a book by the
crook Villon, or the classical Greek
Cavafy; Yea, my poetical desiring is
queer and fleeting. Randomly, I think
of a variety: the grumpy sorceress
Moore, or the gorgeously enflamed
Césaire, or the sassy commie Dalton,
or the wacky virtuoso Di Giorgio, say,
from Uruguay, where I spent my youth
and later went back, as fate would play,
to work as a gym instructor at the
YMCA. Which makes me think, I don't
know why; I've wondered it before, and
my wondering, aye, again is envisioned:

Shouldn't certain U.S. poets stop mooching
on State-sponsored tours in Stalinist China,
where numerous poets are imprisoned?
And now a meditation concerning Japan, if
I may: Is it uncouth (which rhymes above
with youth) for an ex-Trot WASP, like me,
to propound that the minimalist stuff of an
itinerant, alcoholic, apolitical, Meiji-Taishō
Zen haikuist is way more profound and
universal than any prototypical Academic-
Po-Cult-Capital-Speculation fluff?

1.

No doubt it is (uncouth), but hold on,
Mongrel Coalition, why is my heart
skipping beats, is this ventricular fibrillation?
Alright, now it's stopped. Hot men
and women of all colors go back to
baring hot bodies at the waterpark
with their breasts and bikini bottoms.
Is that bad to say, Stasi Po-police of
today? Au contraire, I declare. I mean,
look at that taut ass – is Desire not a radical
Good? Around her/him all that is solid
melts into air. But to return to my subject,
from this metal and rubber reclining chair:
I've been reading Taneda Santōka's bone-
marrow-haiku by this pool, in Wisconsin
Dells. I'm to give an out-loud reading
tomorrow, at a water park resort, believe
it or not (another one down the road – there
are quite a few of them here, right off I-90).
It's sponsored by the Wisconsin Dells
Acker Poetry Belles, you will scarcely
believe it. I'm really quite enjoying being
here, among the Packer crowd, before the
shtick, sipping an Old Fashioned, the third
or fourth, I admit, though some kids with
green and gold life-preserver bubbles on
their stick-like limbs are screaming very
loud before their childhood dies and rots
away, like Emma Bovary's, and the world,
as well; it's like the empty, translucent
shells of Ashbery's cicadas: They can't do

anything about it, nor can you. Why does
the blue jet of liquid jet into the blue?

2.

Anyway, Santōka was writing in the
late Twenties and, yes, he was in his
late twenties, then, too; the haiku
Field was riven by infidel revolt:
It was Haiku-Dada-Time, one could
say. All the vanguard Japanese poets
were young and it was like there was a
mad dash to immolate their youths on
command from some vengeful blue-
liquid-jet God in the *Man'yōshū*, and
then whoosh, youth's season was gone
in a flash. That's how life is, kids, no
rhyme or reason, deep down beneath sad
biology. So would you please just keep it
down, I'm trying to write something about

3.

ideology. OK, forget it. At any rate,
there were, like, huge, blinding flashes
in the sky that had never been
experienced before by human
beings. And then the New American
Poetry appeared all of a sudden,
or so it seemed, to the people in
their twenties standing there,
amazed, within it. They too were
very young and full of life, as life
was full of them. Not that things didn't
happen in the Thirties and Forties:
There was Gertrude Stein writing
speeches for Pétain; the Fugitives
took their stand for slavery; Pound
was screaming darkly in Italy; dark

4.

antennae began to get densely
planted on round summits; tons of
kids got washed out of turrets with
hoses at waterparks in Pushkin's
Russia and Rilke's Prussia, and so
forth and so on. But the New Americans
were the loaded gunners and a half in
follow-up, for sure: They went
bonkers against poetry getting mixed
up with Academic Institutions and
State and corporate money and
slavish position-jockeying and
stuff, as it was, back then, in
proto, with the New Critics. They

5.

were stick-in-the-muds, the
New Americans, I guess you
could put it, quasi-Ultra types,
party poopers, some might opine,
not hip at all on cash bars at
MLA-time and like-Academic
decorum. Say what you want about
their anarchist-line and righteous
zealotry, but had it not been for
them, Post-Avant American poetry
would be in ten pickles of trouble
presently, let me tell you, far
from the wild and sovereign and
honorable spirit that guides the
Field today, thank God, against
the careerist and protocoled
rituals we've all so wisely

6.

eschewed. Because, thankfully,
the New Americans showed us
how it's done—how to fashion
scruffy Autonomous Poetic
Zones against the grain of
career-clubby dispensations; how
to defy capitulation; how to
resist the siren suctions of
the Culture Industry, as Emily
Dickinson more or less urged,
in a poem about slave auctions;
how to refuse being a pawn in the
Rules of the Game; how to forbear
being a species of courtier. Phew!
True, granted, the French/Belgian
Surrealists and the Mexico City
Infrarrealists and the Black Arts

7.

axis helped us to refine our praxis
(so what, we're internationalists,
we don't care who came up with
the key ideas, we don't have to
pretend *we* own it all). And not that
it's all sunny skies at the waterpark,
to coin a phrase, because, sure,
there are two or three sell-outs, still,
hanging around, pretending they're
insurrectionists; you'll always have
a few lame apples in the bushel; that
kind of outlier aberration is assumed:
It's one of those Rules of the Game,
as we know post-Husserl.

8.

So all in all, we're in luck: For were it
not for the New American Poetry, we
Post-Avant American poets would, if
you think about it, possibly be the
laughingstock of Literary History two
hundred years from now(!), like those
Georgians or Firesides or New Critics we
mock today, with their enormous beards
and muttonchops so big you could muck
around in there for a week, like Hansel
and Gretel at the AWP, just to get eaten
by the Witch of Fuck. Sorry, I mean those
ancient guys who thought they were so

9.

avant-garde and all that, when
really they were totally funky
bunkum? Can you imagine *us*
ending up that way, as a group
or period, our architecture all
antique looking, with slender or
thick postmodern columns, and
wall surfaces with pilasters and
decorative features, including
sculpted déjà vu figurines in
frozen, Mannerist pirouettes at
the top of the edifice? Well,
thankfully, we've learned key
lessons from the New American
poetry! These kids won't shut up,
dammit, but kids will be kids, it's
not like their screaming means
they'll be timid bourgeois sell-outs
when they get old, they're just
kids. But I wish the green and gold
bubble-devices around their arms
would pop all at once, that would be
fun, and give some drama to this ersatz

10.

Wave Pool. No, just kidding. I
don't really want any kids to
drown. They are so blithely
content, rising and falling, there,
innocent as the soon-dead day,
which now spreads overhead,
magnificent, its orange and mauve
gown. It's like there's been a
traumatic shipwreck but everyone
is ecstatic. Keep looking up, I say,
and don't look down. So, OK, that's
enough from me: Let us now give thanks
to the New American poetry.

Could Someone Tell Me Why

—para mis ex-amigos poetas

Could someone tell me why I've never been
selected for the yearly *Best American Poetry*?
I'll tell you this: It seriously dills my pickle.
I have written lots of poems, and I know
that many of them have been among the best
in all American poetry. At least for that year.
Sometimes it seems like *everyone* has had a
poem in the *Best American Poetry*. Except
for me. Yeah, it puts my knickers in a knot.
It's not like I don't have connections to the
Best American Poetry. In fact, in the 2006
edition of the *Best American Poetry*, chosen
by Robert Bly, David Villon, in his Preface,
spends a full page talking about me, and he
calls me "incontrovertibly brilliant." You can
look it up, on page IV, I think. After that, I did
emails with David Villon, who of course is
Editor of the *Best American Poetry*. In fact, the
Series was his 1988 idea, so naturally he edits
it. I've read many poems in the *Best American
Poetry* by friends of mine in the poetry world.
Well, that's not really exact. I have read many
poems in the *Best American Poetry* by *former*
friends of mine. I don't know why they're not
friends any longer. It's not that I couldn't know
if I set my mind to thinking on it, it's that I don't
want to think on it, because I know it will make me
more bothered than a mule with a mouthful of bees.
But one thing I can say for damn straight sure:
They are not *former* because they were in the *Best
American Poetry* and I wasn't. I am many things,
but I'm no petty-ass Bobby Sue, that much I swear.
This is because I have resolute confidence in my own

talents. I know for a fact that many a poem of mine should've been selected for the *Best American Poetry*. That all this ungodly time's gone by without a single one of my poems getting picked is spookier than the ghost of Helen Adam at the foot of your canopied bed, holding up the severed, teeth-clacking head of Ezra Pound, say. But on the other hand, it's become a kind of point of manly pride for me. In a corner of my room are all the editions of *Best American Poetry*, stacked in a tower, like a sculpture by Donald Judd, or Carl Chartier, the likely murderer of my fav artist, Ana Mendieta. Except it doesn't emit any light. It is just a dark tower, and in its darkness the poems of my former friends just sit there, waiting. I have often meditated on this matter: Does a poem go on existing even if it's not being read? Does its meter, let's say, still measure? What really happens to a poem, while it sits closed in the dark of a closed book? Do spirits live there? Are there sperm-like, invisible strings that stretch back from them to other poems from hundreds or thousands of years ago that have been lost, but which keep spawning poems? Oh, it makes me feel like I'm about to have a dying duck fit. Also, as years go by, I keep coming across more and more bios in the back of the *Denver Review* that say the poet whose bio I am reading has been published in the *Best American Poetry*. I guess this makes sense, since the more the years go on, and the more aged I become, the more likely it is I will come across poets who have been published in *Best American Poetry*. Yeah, so some of the people who were my former friends are now dead. I feel bad about that, but then I think to myself, Hey, life is short and at least you were

published in the *Best American Poetry*! No, I don't
really mean that, just kidding, I've never thought that,
and never would I. Anyway, as I was saying, David
Villon wrote about me on page IV of his Introduction
to *Best American Poetry of 1999*. (I had written 2006
above, but I just checked, and it was seven years before
that, more proof, when you think of it, that many of
"mis ex-amigos" are dead.) So then I wrote David
Villon over email, which was still a novelty back then,
preceded by dial-up 14th century Poets-in-Hell screams,
and I thanked him very much for saying I was "brilliant,"
but I also mocked him in my email for stating I was the
Author of an apocryphal book I was simply executor for,
proceeding to tell him he was mighty dense about it all,
I think I used that word. Go sit in the truck! I said. I can't
remember what else I said, but it was enough for him to
write back and tell me the KGB reading he had invited
me to give one month from then, all expenses paid, was
cancelled. After more dial-up screeches, I gaily replied,
Hey, sugar, don't let your bulldog mouth overload your
hummingbird ass. Well, that's another former friend from
Best American Poetry down the Tubes of Time, as they say.
Life is so strange. One minute all the chairs have their backs
turned toward the sun and you're getting these feelings of
exaltation, and then two hours later, or whatever, you feel, I
don't know, like all covered in junk and seedy, and you get
very weepy for what seemed like the pleasant early years, it
seems there's little consistency to life, this is how it goes,
day to day. Especially when you've got MS, but even if
you don't, you know what I mean? Speaking of the *Denver
Review*, I received once a formal apology letter from Láird
Vallée, the former editor, because they'd published a poem,
in 2015, I think it was, by a prominent poet who died soon

after that, the poem being an indisputable plagiarism of a
poem I'd published years before, "33 Rules for Poets 23
and Under." One of the things that got me so hopping mad
I could have chewed nails and spit out a barbed wire fence
was that this was maybe my topmost popular poem ever,
printed in a book from Iowa on teaching poetry and widely
used in numerous workshops of Creative Writing over the
course of sundry semesters. Many a young poet, from Bard
to Southeast Missouri State University, has written most
amiably to thank me for it. And then the poached poem
by this notable poet was chosen for inclusion in the *Best
American Poetry* in 2016. Well, you can imagine. I was
so stirred up, I was ready to burn thunderwood and jump
damn salty. Actually, it's funny, but this now reminds me
of something else that makes my butt want to grind corn.
I think it was 2008, and Forêt Raguyer, a former friend,
with whom I'd translated and trekked far and long, called
me on my flip-cell, as I was finishing a fine, satisfied meal
of grits and Spam. He was reading at the Geraldine Dodge
Festival with a bunch of other successful poets, nearly all
of whom, yeah, had been in *Best American Poetry* more
times than Sundays in a year. Wassup, you diamond in a
rhinestone world, I said. Are you US Poet Laureate yet?
Well, he said, I'm in a huge tent at a reading by Noémi
Valois, the best known Arab-American poet, and she
just brought the fucking place down with a naked filch
of your poem "Baghdad Exceeds Its Object." Say *what?*
I said. Yep, I swear on a stack of 19th century Virginia
Bibles, he said, with some excited anachronism. Well,
I said, that sure makes me madder than a Wampus Cat in a
rainstorm. I'll be goddamned. A few months later, when
Forêt Raguyer was writing for the Poetry Foundation blog,
he posted this famous Arab-American poet's anti-war poem

next to mine and invited readers to compare for themselves.
Fifty or sixty people wrote in to say how obvious it was.
And wouldn't you know: Why the poem by this plagiarist
poet ended up in the *Best American Poetry* of 2009. Oh,
I was tetchier than a jumpin' frog 'neath a wet settin' hen.
Also, once I read in NYC with David L'Amaury, one of my
fav poets when I was a teen. This was after that bout
with David Villon, Editor of the *Best American Poetry*,
so of course he didn't come (*secundum* Pierre Bourdieu).
But Jacques Marchand, an unwell blogger, back in the
aughts, who'd been in *Best American Poetry* twice, was
there. I asked him after the reading why he wrote a letter
to my college President, urging, no lie, that I should be
fired forthwith. I said, So, Jacques Marchand, I will say
I am so mad at you I could jump out of my pants. And in
fact, I am so righteous livid, Monsieur, that I am thinking
of taking off your *own* pants, and hanging you with them
by your left foot from a lamppost, you homunculus elf. I
can't recall what Jacques Marchand said, but he fell quite
ill at ease during this tête-à-tête, very different than his
"macho" online pose, back in those days, as an *enfant
terrible* of the blogs, when he'd post cute photos of his
penis poking up out of his briefs. David L'Amaury and I
hugged and said goodbye, and that was the last time
I ever saw him, though we continued to correspond
over email, until he became quite upset over my book
about Frank O'Hara and Kenneth Koch, the one that
suggests that maybe Koch wrote one of O'Hara's most
famous poems, for which I received a lawsuit threat from
Random House, signed by Jordanie Lurens, Rony Moreau,
Guillaume Gossain, and Antonin Cotin, amazingly enough,
all who'd been, seven times each, in *Best American Poetry*.
Oh, that made me madder than a boiled owl. And I right

said they'd better give their dark hearts to Jesus, because
their butts were mine, and then I never heard from them
again—even after the *Times Literary Supplement* named
the book a "TLS Book of the Year." And you know what?
David Villon then wrote an article on his *Best American
Poetry* blog about how Kenneth Koch couldn't have written
the poem I said he might have because Koch's ego was too
big and he never would have been able to keep it a secret.
Let me tell you, that made me hotter than the rattlesnake
that married the garden hose. But then again, I just don't
know. Why does this happen to me, what is it about me
that makes me lose all my friends, it's really starting
to afflict me. And now that I think of it, maybe all these
things are connected to why I am not in *Best American
Poetry*, maybe I bring it on myself, causing Charles Delille,
for example, to write hurting things about me in essays, or
Ronald Voiture, who seemed to like me well enough when
in Leningrad, when we were there together, though then, in
the group-promo book he co-authored shortly afterwards about
the experience, titled *Leningrad*, he called me and my two
blameless friends who were with me "American cockroaches,"
which sticks in my craw like hair on a half-cooked biscuit. But
that's OK, I've gotten back at him plenty for that in the years
since, exposing him for the charlatan he is a few times, or so I
like to think. But maybe he has the last laugh, because he's in
Best American Poetry twelve years in a row, and I'm at zero.
Which reminds me that once I read at Buffalo, invited by
Étienne de Navarre, a nice book collector and head of Buffalo
Poetics Program, who's been in the *Best American Poetry*
five times, though he's from Canada, and before the reading
we went out to a bar and he says to me, You know, Kent,
Marjorie Arouét phoned two days ago from Pacific Palisades,
and said, Why on earth did you ask the horrid Kent Johnson

to come and read at Buffalo, what the hell is wrong with you?
Say *what*? I said. She *really said that*? Gosh all Hemlock.
Yep, he said, I swear on my *Lolita* and *Prufrock*, both signed.
Later that evening I read to maybe fifty mostly grad students,
and because my glasses had broken on the trip there, I had to
read with my prescription Ray-Bans, so in this gorgeous rare-
books library I looked both cool-cat and crazy as a wombat.
And because I was mad as a three-legged dog trying to bury
a turd on a frozen pond, I read really fast and good. Most
of the audience was young Conceptual poets, celebrants
of Kerman Lalond and Venus de Kristees, this being about a
year before the former did his Michael Brown autopsy bomb
at Brown, a University founded on money made through
the slave trade, though that doesn't seem to bother vanguard
poets, and I boldly read a nasty suite that lampooned ConPo
for the scam it was. When I was done, some of these hip
Conceptual grad students invited me out for drinks and we
had a swell time. And I've always wondered: Isn't it strange
how no matter what, like during temporary cease fires in
WWI, people who have been launching poison gas at each
other can come out of the trenches and dance together and
share chocolates and things and then return to their trenches
and start launching poison gas again? And then the sun and
the moon and the stars and stuff cover the quiet field, which
is now full of trees and grass and is a memorial, a sacred
place, where people come to think and read or just remember
the people that they loved, even if they thought they didn't
when they were younger, then, when they were impulsive,
mysterious, and sad. I know poetry is life and death, and I
could go on for the length of a book about this stuff, because
I've had a whole run of it. But I'm ready to stop, now, and just
ask the voiceless, simple air, because I really want to know,
Could someone tell me why?

CPSIA information can be obtained
at www.ICGtesting.com
Printed in the USA
BVHW031259231120
594012BV00008B/79